Ronaldinho

The Complete Story
of a Football Superstar

100+ Interesting Trivia Questions, Interactive
Activities, and Random, Shocking Fun Facts Every
"Ronaldinho" Fan Needs to Know

HOUSE OF BALLERS

YOUR FREE BONUS!

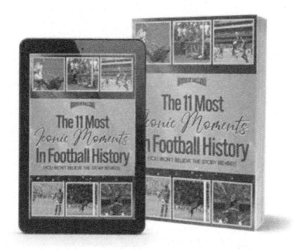

The 11 Most Iconic Moments in Football History

In this special edition, you'll discover the secret stories behind some of football's most memorable, hilarious, and shocking moments.

Enjoy!

>>SCAN THE QR CODE BELOW TO GAIN EXCLUSIVE ACCESS<<

CONTENTS

INTRODUCTION

He was the greatest footballer and entertainer of all time! Ronaldo de Assis Moreira, aka Ronaldinho Gaucho, or simply Ronaldinho, is instantly recognizable as one of the most skillful attacking players in the history of football. A fine exponent of Joga Bonito, Ronaldinho made many people fall in love with football during his heydays.

Armed with an armory of impossible-to-defend, five-star skill moves, it was a futile endeavor to try to stop the gap-toothed Brazilian. At a point in his career, he debuted new skill moves every match. From stadiums such as Old Trafford to the Santiago Bernabeu, opposing fans roared their approval for his style of play.

His career arc was not surprising to those who knew him as a young kid. "Little Ronaldo" was born into a family of football players, and he had to deal with poverty and the loss of his father at an early age. Luckily for Dinho, he dazzled and amazed as a youth player on the pitch.

He enjoyed a celebrated youth career, including winning the 1999 FIFA Under-17 World Cup and the Bronze Ball at the tournament. Like his elder brother Roberto, Ronaldinho played for Gremio for a few years before moving to PSG. But it was during Brazil's victorious outing at the 2002 FIFA World Cup that Ronaldinho truly announced his arrival to the limelight with three assists and two goals, including a spectacular 40-yard free-kick against England in the quarterfinal.

His popularity only soared higher after he moved to Barcelona in 2003, and he instantly established himself as one of the best footballers in the world at the time. He helped Barcelona end a six-year title wait in 2005 and led the club to a La Liga and UEFA Champions League double in 2006. He won consecutive FIFA World Player of the Year Awards in 2004 and 2005 and the European Footballer of the Year Award in 2005. Ronaldinho is the only player in history to win the FIFA World Cup, UEFA Champions League, Copa America, Copa Libertadores, and Ballon d'Or, and one of only nine players that have won the FIFA World Cup, UEFA Champions League, and the Ballon d'Or.

Ronaldinho had a great first touch, vision, passing, playmaking capability, shooting, and expertise in dead-ball situations. He was also top of the class for his flair, technical skills, dribbling ability, and close ball control.

Unfortunately, Ronaldinho's time at the top fizzled out a bit prematurely. Nevertheless, even after leaving Barcelona, Ronaldinho secured landmark trophies for his new clubs. His trademark hairstyle sent shivers down opponents' ends, and his mere presence on the pitch generated an aura of invisibility.

What made Ronaldinho tick?

Why was he nicknamed "little Ronaldo?"

Is it true that he scored 23 goals in one game?

Is it true that he was arrested and jailed for a month?

Get the answers to these and many more questions in this trivia book. In the following eight chapters, we will look at the career of one of the most recognizable icons of modern football. As an attacker, Ronaldinho was the player most young footballers aspired to be. He wore a smile permanently as he destroyed defenses, but more importantly, he influenced a whole generation of footballers.

Find out more about Ronaldinho in the next chapters, happy reading!

CHAPTER

1

EARLY LIFE

"I come from a family where football has always been present, my uncles my father and my brother were all players. Living with that background, I learned a great deal from them. I tried to devote myself to it more and more with the passage of time."
- Ronaldinho

Ronaldo de Assis Moreira, aka Ronaldinho Gaucho, or simply Ronaldinho, was born on March 21, 1980 in Porto Alegre, Brazil. His father, Joao de Assis Moreira, played football for the local club, Esporte Clube Cruzeiro, and was a welder at a shipyard. At the same time, his mother, Dona Miguelina Eloi Assis dos Santos, was a cosmetic saleswoman before becoming a nurse. Before he retired from football, Ronaldinho's father worked as a matchday doorman at the Brazilian top-flight club Gremio.

Ronaldinho has a sister named Deisy, who was his biggest fan and handled his PR duties when he turned professional, and a brother named Roberto de Assis Moreira, who also played football at Gremio. The club even offered Ronaldinho's family comfortable accommodation to keep Roberto on their books. However, when he suffered a severe knee injury, Roberto's dreams of becoming a footballer at the highest level were crushed. He went on to manage his brother's career as an advisor, agent, and role model.

Ronaldinho attended Colegio Santa Teresa de Jesus. He inherited his family's passion for football and began playing the game at an amateur level at age seven. He spent most of his childhood in one-on-one training sessions with his brother Roberto, who was the first to recognize Ronaldinho's potential talent and act on it by creating daily training sessions for him. He would take his junior brother onto the field after his practice session or sometimes skip his sessions to train his little brother.

Sadly, Ronaldinho's father passed away after he had turned eight. With the help of his brother Roberto, who has set aside his fledgling career to cater to the family, he continued to improve. He was given the nickname "Ronaldinho," which meant "small Ronaldo," early in his youth career as he was often the smallest and youngest player in youth team matches. Ronaldinho also began playing futsal in his early teens, which helped him develop certain aspects of his game, like quick reactions and close ball control.

Ronaldinho first came into the limelight when he scored all 23 goals in a 23-0 win for his youth side; at 13 years of age. A few years later, he received a call-up to the Brazil Under-17 side, whom he helped win the 1997 FIFA Under-17 World Championship in Egypt. He scored two goals at the tournament, both coming from penalty kicks, as his team went all the way to emerge as champions. Growing up, Ronaldinho idolized his father, Brazil's 1970 World Cup-winning star Rivelino, Diego Maradona, Romario, and his two future teammates Rivaldo and Ronaldo, with whom he formed a fearsome attacking triumvirate that led Brazil to FIFA World Cup glory in 2002.

10 Trivia questions

1. On what day was Ronaldinho born?

    A. March 20, 1982

    B. March 21, 1980

    C. March 22, 1982

    D. March 23, 1980

2. How many siblings does Ronaldinho have?

    A. 0

    B. 1

    C. 2

    D. 3

3. At which of these clubs did Ronaldinho's father work as a doorman?

    A. Botafogo

    B. Cruzeiro

    C. Internacional

    D. Gremio

4. At 13, how many goals did Ronaldinho famously score in a 23-0 win for his side?

    A. 23

    B. 22

    C. 21

    D. 20

5. How many goals did Ronaldinho score at the 1997 FIFA Under-17 Championship?

    A. 3

    B. 2

    C. 1

    D. 0

6. Which Argentine World Cup-winning star did Ronaldinho idolize?

    A. Mario Kempes

    B. Jorge Burruchaga

    C. Diego Maradona

    D. Daniel Pasarella

7. Which club gifted Ronaldinho's family a house?

    A. Fluminense

    B. Santos

    C. São Paulo

    D. Gremio

8. In which Brazilian city was Ronaldinho born?

    A. Porto Alegre

    B. Rio de Janeiro

    C. Curitiba

    D. Fortaleza

9.   How old was Ronaldinho when his father died?

  A. 6

  B. 8

  C. 11

  D. 10

10. Which Brazil 1994 World Cup-winning star did Ronaldinho idolize?

  A. Dunga

  B. Bebeto

  C. Romario

  D. Branco

10 Trivia Answers

1. B – March 21, 1980

2. C – 2

3. D – Gremio

4. A – 23

5. B – 2

6. C – Diego Maradona

7. D – Gremio

8. A – Porto Alegre

9. B - 8

10. C – Romario

RONALDINHO MAZE #1

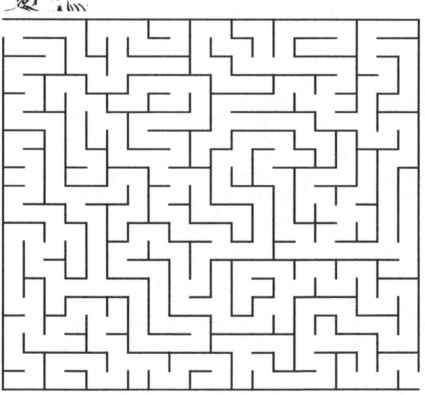

GOAL

CHAPTER

2

START OF PROFESSIONAL CAREER

"I've worked with some great players in my time, and all at a very interesting period in their careers, nineteen to twenty years old. But, with due respect to others, Ronaldinho was a cut above the rest."

– Celso Roth

L ike his elder brother, Ronaldinho came through Gremio's youth academy. Following his heroics with the Brazil Under-17 team at the 1997 FIFA Under-17 World Championship in Egypt, he was promoted to the senior squad and given his first professional contract. He debuted his first team in a 1-0 Copa Libertadores win over Vasco de Gama in 1998. A year later, he had his breakthrough season. Dinho scored 22 goals in 47 games and displayed eye-catching performances in derbies against Internacional, most prominently in the Rio Grande do Sul State Championship final (Campeonato Gaucho) on June 20, 1999. Ronaldinho's match-winning display included a flick of the ball over the head of Brazil's 1994 FIFA World Cup-winning captain, Dunga, leaving the veteran flat-footed after a mazy dribble in another move. Ronaldinho enjoyed more success with Gremio after the club emerged as the inaugural winners of the Copa Sul. Between 1998 and 2001, he made 125 appearances across all competitions for Gremio and scored 58 goals.

North London club Arsenal showed interest in acquiring Ronaldinho in 2001. The transfer was unsuccessful due to the inability to secure a work permit. This happened because of Ronaldinho's status as a non-EU player who had not played an appreciable number of international games. Dinho then considered moving to the Scottish side St. Mirren. However, that transfer was also deemed unsuccessful due to his involvement in a fake passport debacle in Brazil. Ronaldinho finally sealed a move to French Ligue 1 side Paris Saint-Germain for €5 million. He was given jersey number 21 and included in a squad that consisted of compatriot Aloisio, Nicolas Anelka, and skillful Nigerian midfielder Austin Jay-Jay Okocha.

Ronaldinho made his Ligue 1 debut on August 4, 2001, coming on as a substitute in a 1-1 draw against Auxerre. He was in and out of the starting lineup for most of the early parts of the 2001-02 season and scored his first goal for the club in a 2-2 draw against Lyon on October 13. In the same match against Lyon, he converted a penalty on the 79th minute to level the game at 2-2, ten minutes after he had been introduced as a substitute. After the winter break, Ronaldinho went on a four-game scoring spree, finding the back of the net in games against Monaco, Rennes, Lens, and Lorient in early 2002. On March 16, he netted a brace in PSG's 3-1 win over Troyes, and scored his last league goal of the season in a 2-0 victory over Metz on April 27. He also played a pivotal role in the club's run to the semifinals of the Coupe de la Ligue that season, scoring two goals in the round of 16 tie against Guingamp after he had been introduced as a half-time substitute. He finished his first season at the club with 13 goals in 40 appearances across all competitions, with nine of his goals coming in 28 Ligue 1 appearances. Despite his satisfactory performances on the pitch, Ronaldinho incurred the wrath of then PSG manager Luis Fernandez, who claimed that the Brazilian sensation was too carried away with the Parisian nightlife to the detriment of his focus on football; and that he always returned late from holidays in Brazil.

Despite the fallout with Fernandez, Ronaldinho continued at PSG in the 2002-03 season and better yet, received jersey number 10, which had recently become vacant following the transfer of Okocha to English Premier League side Bolton Wanderers. On October 26, 2002, Ronaldinho bagged a brace in a 3-1 home win over fierce rivals Marseille. The first of his two goals came from a free-kick that curled beyond a wall of Marseille players standing inside their penalty box. He scored another goal in a 3-0 win at Marseille in the return fixture, running half the length of the pitch before dinking the ball over Marseille keeper Vedran Runje. On February 22, 2004, Ronaldinho scored what turned out to be the goal of the season in a game against Guingamp. After receiving the ball, he beat one opponent, then made a one-two with a teammate to beat a second opponent, lifted the ball over the head of a third, and beat a fourth with a step-over before he dispatched the ball into the net by dinking it over the keeper.

Ronaldinho was also lauded for his display in the Coupe de France that season, scoring both of his team's goals in a 2-0 win over Bordeaux in the semifinal of the competition. After scoring the opener in the 21st minute, Ronaldinho capped off a fine display with a lobbed effort that floated over Bordeaux keeper Ulrich Rame. PSG fell to a 2-1 defeat to Auxerre in the final and finished a disappointing 11th on the Ligue 1 table at the end of the season. Ronaldinho, who had scored 12 goals in 35 appearances across all competitions, declared that he wanted a move away from the club. His stay at PSG ended with 25 goals in 77 appearances across all competitions.

10 Trivia questions

1. When did Ronaldinho make his Gremio first-team debut?

   A. 1996

   B. 1997

   C. 1998

   D. 1999

2. In which of these competitions did Ronaldinho make his first appearance for Gremio?

   A. Copa do Brazil

   B. Campeonato Brasileiro Serie A

   C. Copa Sul

   D. Copa Libertadores

3. How many goals did Ronaldinho score during his time at Gremio?

   A. 39

   B. 58

   C. 47

   D. 66

4. How many appearances did Ronaldinho make in his spell with Gremio?

   A. 125

   B. 120

   C. 115

   D. 105

5. What was Ronaldinho's jersey number upon arrival at PSG?

   A. 10

   B. 11

   C. 21

   D. 27

6. How much did it cost PSG to sign Ronaldinho from Gremio?

   A. €8 million

   B. €7 million

   C. €6 million

   D. €5 million

7. Which opponent did Ronaldinho face on his Ligue 1 debut?

   A. Auxerre

   B. Bordeaux

   C. Bastia

   D. Guingamp

8. Who were the opponents when Ronaldinho scored his first PSG goal?

   A. Lens

   B. Lyon

   C. Lorient

   D. Troyes

9. How many league goals did Ronaldinho score in his first season at PSG?

   A. 12

   B. 10

   C. 9

   D. 8

10. Ronaldinho scored the 2002-03 Ligue 1 Goal of the Season. Who were the opponents? against which team?

    A. Sochaux

    B. Nantes

    C. Le Havre

    D. Guingamp

10 Trivia Answers

1. C – 1998

2. D – Copa Libertadores

3. B – 58

4. A – 125

5. C – 21

6. D - €5 million

7. A – Auxerre

8. B – Lyon

9. C – 9

10. D – Guingamp

RONALDINHO WORD SEARCH #1

```
E  H  I  H  E  O  S  G  L  I  C  A  M  P  N  O  U  N  R  Y
C  V  M  W  R  G  W  Z  C  C  H  P  C  Q  W  B  K  O  Y  P
W  X  N  D  P  Z  Q  O  L  Y  Q  S  U  L  A  H  U  X  K  B
C  O  C  G  C  O  R  A  D  K  F  N  Q  S  E  R  I  E  A  F
H  O  U  Z  R  R  K  M  X  P  L  A  L  E  Y  E  K  W  F  I
A  I  D  A  L  B  J  O  N  Q  O  X  I  W  I  N  G  E  R  R
M  I  D  W  N  I  B  A  L  L  O  N  D  O  R  D  J  J  G  J
P  D  S  L  N  A  Q  C  J  C  J  T  O  X  F  B  I  F  J  G
I  V  L  D  K  F  P  N  Z  A  Q  M  I  M  I  E  I  I  L  I
O  B  H  J  F  W  K  D  L  I  X  J  Z  R  M  M  N  W  I  J
N  L  A  L  I  G  A  P  G  L  J  C  A  T  F  I  B  J  V  F
S  Z  M  E  Z  D  T  K  W  C  R  H  H  L  T  Q  J  L  Q  K
L  K  H  A  D  F  V  M  E  U  A  J  V  S  A  N  S  I  R  O
E  O  P  N  R  O  N  A  L  D  I  N  H  O  O  R  Q  D  P  W
A  V  Z  F  X  W  J  Y  I  T  M  R  O  S  S  O  N  E  R  I
G  S  Q  N  O  B  U  U  X  Y  E  O  S  A  Z  E  T  F  S  I
U  T  Z  P  B  R  A  Z  I  L  W  H  O  L  W  E  Y  E  L  W
E  X  N  H  U  T  W  T  E  S  C  O  N  S  K  X  N  I  P  U
A  J  J  K  K  V  N  T  E  J  V  W  A  R  T  J  V  P  Q  Q
W  C  X  O  W  L  U  O  L  X  W  E  T  J  P  O  K  G  S  E
```

RONALDINHO	SERIEA	WINGER
ROSSONERI	SANSIRO	LALIGA
CAMPNOU	BRAZIL	BALLONDOR
CHAMPIONSLEAGUE		

CHAPTER

3

FIFA WORLD CUP GLORY

"On the eve of the final, Ronaldo, Rivaldo, and Ronaldinho warmed up in the Yokohama Stadium by merrily trying to out-wizard each other in the Japanese drizzle."

– Amy Lawrence

Ronaldinho's acquaintance with international football began in 1997 when he was included in the Brazil Under-17 team that won the 1997 South American Under-17 Championship, where he made seven appearances and scored one goal. A few months later, he was included in the Brazil Under-17 side that won the 1997 FIFA Under-17 World Championship in Egypt. He made six appearances at the tournament, and his two goals were scored from penalty kicks against Austria in the group stage, and Germany in the semifinals. He was awarded the Bronze Ball as the competition's third-best player.

In 1999, Ronaldinho scored three goals in nine appearances to help Brazil's Under-20 team to a third-place finish at the 1999 South American U-20 Championship. At the 1999 FIFA World Youth Championship, Ronaldinho made five appearances and scored his first goal of the tournament in Brazil's last group game against Zambia, which ended in a 5-1 win for his side. In the round of 16 games against Croatia, Ronaldinho netted a first-half brace to help Brazil to a 4-0 victory before his team crashed out of the tournament following a 2-1 defeat to Uruguay in the quarterfinals.

Ronaldinho made his senior international debut on June 26, 1999, in a 3-0 win over Latvia in a friendly game. He was included in Brazil's squad for the 1999 Copa America, where he made four appearances and scored his only goal of the tournament in Brazil's 7-0 rout against Venezuela in their opening game. Brazil cruised to a sixth Copa America title by winning all of their remaining five games at the tournament.

A week after the completion of the 1999 Copa America, Ronaldinho was included in Brazil's squad for the 1999 FIFA Confederation Cup, a tournament in which he would score a goal each in group stage games against Germany, the USA, and New Zealand, as well as a hattrick in the 8-2 rout versus Saudi Arabia in the semifinals. The only game Ronaldinho did not score in was the final, which Brazil lost 4-3 to Mexico. Regardless, he was voted as the tournament's best player and awarded the Golden Ball, and he also picked up the Golden Boot after finishing as joint-top goal scorer with 6 goals.

In 2000, Ronaldinho scored Brazil's third goal in a 7-0 rout of Thailand in a friendly game before he led Brazil's Under-23 side to glory at the South American Pre-Olympics tournament, scoring nine goals in seven matches. At the Summer Olympics football event in September 2000, he made four appearances and scored his only goal of the tournament in Brazil's 2-1 defeat to eventual winners Cameroon in the quarterfinals. Ronaldinho also made six scoreless appearances in the 2002 FIFA World Cup qualification series between 2001 and 2002.

On March 3, 2001, Ronaldinho scored the opening goal of a 2-1 win over the USA in a friendly game. He also scored the equalizer during a 1-1 draw with Portugal on April 17, 2002. He was named in Brazil's 23-man squad for the 2002 FIFA World Cup, where he played in five of Brazil's seven games at the tournament, forming a fearsome attacking triumvirate with Rivaldo and Ronaldo, which the media labeled the "Three Rs," and was already on display in Brazil's victorious outing at the 1999 Copa America.

Ronaldinho's first goal at the 2002 FIFA World Cup came from a first-half penalty in a 4-0 win over China in the second group stage game. His other goal, one of the most memorable in FIFA World Cup history, came from a 40-yard free-kick in a 2-1 comeback win over England in the quarterfinal. Besides his two goals at the tournament, he provided three assists, including one for Rivaldo for the equalizer against England. Ronaldinho was sent off seven minutes after his goal against England for a foul on Danny Mills, forcing him to sit out Brazil's 1-0 semifinal win over Turkey. He was restored to the starting lineup for Brazil's 2-0 win over Germany in the final.

10 Trivia questions

1. How many goals did Ronaldinho score at the 1997 South American U-17 Championship?

   A. 0

   B. 2

   C. 1

   D. 3

2. How many appearances did Ronaldinho make at the 1997 FIFA Under-17 Championship?

   A. 6

   B. 5

   C. 4

   D. 3

3. How many goals did Ronaldinho score at the 1999 South American U-20 Championship?

   A. 6

   B. 5

   C. 4

   D. 3

4. Ronaldinho scored his first goal at the 1999 FIFA World Youth Championship against _____?

   A. Uruguay

   B. Croatia

   C. Zambia

   D. Honduras

5. When did Ronaldinho make his senior international debut?

   A. June 25, 1998

   B. June 26, 1999

   C. June 27, 1997

   D. June 28, 1998

6. Ronaldinho scored his only goal of the 1999 Copa America against_____?

   A. Argentina

   B. Mexico

   C. Chile

   D. Venezuela

7. How many goals did Ronaldinho score at the 1999 FIFA Confederations Cup?

   A. 6

   B. 5

   C. 4

   D. 3

8. How many times did Ronaldinho appear in the 2002 FIFA World Cup qualifiers?

   A. 2

   B. 7

   C. 6

   D. 5

9. Ronaldinho scored his first FIFA World Cup goal against_____?

    A. Turkey

    B. China

    C. Costa Rica

    D. Belgium

10. How many assists did Ronaldinho provide at the 2002 FIFA World Cup?

    A. 3

    B. 4

    C. 5

    D. 6

10 Trivia Answers

1. B – 2

2. A – 6

3. D – 3

4. C – Zambia

5. B – June 26 1999

6. D – Venezuela

7. A – 6

8. C – 6

9. B – China

10. A – 3

RONALDINHO WORD SCRAMBLE #1

1. KLULFLIS ILEBDRBR _____

2. EAIVTERC RASSPE _____

3. YAAMOBTNLF SYLET _____

4. RSRTICTEK NCIGAMIA _____

5. YAPKNLIGAM NSGEUI _____

6. NEBTPEIRDULAC EOSMV _____

7. PES-RLWNGCIDAO SRTCIK _____

8. -CEKRKEIF LAETISSICP _____

9. STSIAS AESTRM _____

10. FUOJYL HSCRMAIA _____

11. ASMBA ILFRA _____

12. TSTNSIAHUCIE ILMSE _____

13. GAOJ IOBTON _____

14. FRELEASS CTRAKTAE _____

15. TLRNAUA MAOWHNS _____

16. IVNIEENTV YPLA _____

17. DFVEEISEN SUEPRSER _____

18. GEEANTL ABLL NCOOLTR _____

19. CUKIQ WOOKOTRF _____

20. GOBLAL NCOI _____

CHAPTER

4

SUPERSTARDOM AND SUCCESSES AT BARCELONA

"The greatest compliment I could give him (Ronaldinho) is that he's given Barcelona our spirit back. He has made us smile again."

– Carles Puyol

In mid-June 2003, news of David Beckham's imminent transfer from Manchester United to Real Madrid came as a bitter blow to newly elected Barcelona president Joan Laporta, who had based the majority of his campaign on the mandate that he would bring the world's most high-profile football player to the Nou Camp. In one of his statements, Laporta commented, "I said we would lead Barca to the forefront of the footballing world, and for that to occur, we had to sign one of these three players, David Beckham, Thierry Henry, or Ronaldinho."

At one point that summer, it seemed Barcelona had won the race to sign Beckham, ahead of their fierce rivals and other top European clubs like Inter and AC Milan. Laporta had agreed a deal with Manchester United for the England captain, but Real Madrid, who had initially refuted rumors linking Beckham with a move to the Spanish capital, swooped to the front of the queue and sealed a deal with both Beckham and Manchester United, ahead of other suitors. With Henry deciding to remain at Arsenal, Barcelona had no other option but to try and sign Ronaldinho, whom Manchester United also coveted as a replacement for Beckham, on their 3-man shortlist.

Barcelona fought off the advances of Manchester United, and secured the signature of Ronaldinho from PSG for €30 million. He was handed jersey number 10 and made his Barcelona debut on July 27, 2003, in a pre-season friendly game against Juventus at Gillette Stadium, Foxborough, Massachusetts. His first official goal for the club came in a La Liga game against Sevilla on September 3, when Ronaldinho received the ball from his keeper in his half of the pitch, ran through the midfield, and dribbled past two opponents before smashing a shot in from 30-yards that went in off the underside of the crossbar.

Barcelona dropped to 12th in the La Liga standings at one point in the 2003-04 season after Ronaldinho picked up an injury in the first half of the season. He regained fitness and scored 15 goals in 32 league appearances to help Barcelona to a second-place finish on the league table. He also provided teammate Xavi Hernandez with a no-look lobbed pass to score the winner in a 2-1 win at fierce rivals Real Madrid towards the end of the season. According to Xavi, Barcelona's first away win at Real in seven years was the catalyst for "the Barcelona rise." At the end of the 2003-04 season, Ronaldinho had 22 goals in 45 appearances across all competitions.

In the 2004-05 season, Ronaldinho helped Barcelona to the La Liga title ahead of rivals Real Madrid, scoring 9 goals in 35 league games. Dinho led Barcelona to the round of 16 in the UEFA Champions League, scoring four goals in seven appearances, including a brace in the 4-2 round of 16 second-leg defeat at Chelsea that sent Barcelona crashing out of the competition following a 5-4 aggregate defeat. At the start of May 2005, Ronaldinho provided a crucial assist for Lionel Messi's first competitive Barcelona goal, conjuring a lobbed pass over the Albacete defense for Messi to apply a dinked finish over the keeper. He won the 2004 FIFA World Player of the Year.

With three years left on the 5-year contract Ronaldinho signed in 2003, he was offered a new nine-year deal worth £85 million over the length of the contract by Barcelona. Instead, Ronaldinho signed a two-year extension in September 2005 that comprised a minimum-fee release clause that gave him the option of exiting Barcelona should another club submit a bid of at least £85 million to Barcelona for the Brazilian winger.

On November 19, 2005, Ronaldinho netted a brace and set up Samuel Eto'o for the third to help Barcelona to a resounding 3-0 win at fierce rivals Real Madrid. His performance was so impressive that he was applauded by Real Madrid fans when he was substituted, making him the second Barcelona player ever to be applauded by Real fans after Diego Maradona in June 1983. He won the 2005 Ballon d'Or, and a few months later added a second consecutive FIFA World Player of the Year award.

Ronaldinho helped Barcelona to a successful defence of the La Liga title in the 2005-06 season, scoring 17 goals in 29 league appearances. He also played a pivotal role in the club's triumphant UEFA Champions League campaign, scoring decisive goals in the round of 16 and quarterfinals against Chelsea, and Benfica, respectively. He also supplied his trademark no-look lobbed assist for teammate Ludovic Giuly to score the only goal of the semi-final tie against AC Milan, as well as the pass that sent Eto'o through on goal in the final, before the striker was impeded by Arsenal goalkeeper Jens Lehmann, who received a straight red card for the infraction. Barcelona came from behind to beat Arsenal 2-1 and seal an impressive La Liga and UEFA Champions League double. Ronaldinho finished the season with 26 goals in 45 appearances across all competitions, including 7 in 12 UEFA Champions League matches.

Ronaldinho scored his 50th career league goal with the first of his two goals against Villareal on November 25, 20006. The second goal was a superb overhead kick goal, which he later admitted to journalists he had dreamt of scoring since he was a child. On December 14, he scored one and provided assists for two other goals in Barcelona's 4-0 FIFA Club World Cup semi-final win over Mexican side, Club America in Yokohama, Japan. He was awarded the tournament's Bronze Ball despite Barcelona's 1-0 loss to Brazilian side, Internacional in the final.

On November 15, Ronaldinho came third in the 2006 FIFA World Player of the Year, behind Zinedine Zidane and Italy's 2006 World Cup-winning captain Fabio Cannavaro, who won the award in addition to the Ballon d'Or he claimed a few months back. Barcelona's defence of the UEFA Champions League came to an end in March 2007, as a 1-0 win at Liverpool could not avert a round of 16 exit after the Merseyside club had won the first leg 2-1 at Camp Nou to advance on the away goals rule.

Ronaldinho picked up a knock in a pulsating 3-3 home draw against Real Madrid, forcing him out of a charity game on March 13. Despite his career-best tally of 21 league goals, Barcelona lost out on a third successive title in the 2006-07 season due to a worse head-to-head record with Real Madrid after both teams finished on the same number of points following the conclusion of the last round of matches in June 2007. Ronaldinho finished the season with 24 goals in 49 appearances across all competitions. Two of his non-league goals came in eight UEFA Champions League appearances, with the third coming in his two appearances at the FIFA Club World Cup.

The 2007-08 season turned out to be Ronaldinho's last at Barcelona. He endured a torrid season, plagued by injury and fitness problems, but still made his 200th career league appearance in a game against Osasuna on February 3, 2008. A hamstring tear on his right leg on April 3 brought a premature end to his season. In what turned out to be his last Barcelona appearance, Ronaldinho and Messi each captained a team of international stars in an anti-racism friendly match in Venezuela on June 28, 2008. Ronaldinho scored two goals and supplied two assists as the game finished in a 7-7 draw. Ronaldinho's Barcelona career ended with 94 goals in 207 appearances across all competitions, which included 70 goals in 145 La Liga games.

10 Trivia questions

1. How much did Barcelona pay to acquire the services of Ronaldinho from PSG?

    A. €30 million

    B. €32.5 million

    C. €35 million

    D. €37.5 million

2. Ronaldinho made his Barcelona debut in a pre-season game. Who were the opponents?

    A. Roma

    B. Inter

    C. AC Milan

    D. Juventus

3. Ronaldinho scored his first competitive goal for Barcelona against_____?

    A. Villareal

    B. Espanyol

    C. Sevilla

    D. Valencia

4. How many league goals did Ronaldinho score in his first season at Barcelona?

   A. 12

   B. 15

   C. 18

   D. 20

5. How many competitive appearances did Ronaldinho make in his first season at Barcelona?

   A. 45

   B. 44

   C. 43

   D. 42

6. How many UEFA Champions League goals did Ronaldinho score in the 2004-05 season?

   A. 7

   B. 6

   C. 5

   D. 4

7. Ronaldinho provided a lobbed assist for a teammate in the 2005-06 UEFA Champions League semi-final. Who was the teammate?

   A. Deco

   B. Mark van Bommel

   C. Ludovic Guily

   D. Xavi Hernandez

8. On the day Ronaldinho scored his 50th career league goal, who were the opponents?

   A. Athletic Bilbao

   B. Villareal

   C. Valencia

   D. Deportivo La Coruna

9. How many goals did Ronaldinho score at the 2006 FIFA Club World Cup?

   A. 1

   B. 2

   C. 3

   D. 4

10. In which season did Ronaldinho score a career-best 21 league goals?

   A. 2007-08

   B. 2006-07

   C. 2005-06

   D. 2004-05

10 Trivia Answers

1. A - €30 million

2. D – Juventus

3. C – Sevilla

4. B – 15

5. A – 45

6. D – 4

7. C – Ludovic Giuly

8. B – Villareal

9. A – 1

10. B – 2006-07

RONALDINHO WORD SEARCH #2

```
Z  A  P  S  I  C  P  L  J  N  Q  B  A  R  C  E  L  O  N  A
L  S  T  L  V  R  Q  U  F  Y  B  S  J  X  T  H  K  X  I  M
X  B  G  U  W  M  S  B  S  Q  P  C  S  G  A  P  L  V  I  F
F  J  P  E  W  N  K  X  S  Z  K  C  A  R  A  T  H  J  L  L
I  C  R  I  G  H  T  F  O  O  T  E  D  J  R  H  Z  G  W  A
P  O  F  O  Y  S  C  S  J  H  X  A  K  P  G  C  U  E  F  M
K  T  G  G  M  Q  F  K  O  X  X  B  A  G  P  Z  G  X  T  E
V  F  P  N  J  M  O  I  S  L  L  N  S  P  T  F  Y  P  T  N
T  O  L  K  Y  F  Q  L  B  I  K  A  S  M  J  V  P  U  Y  G
A  O  C  X  I  D  N  L  J  X  S  D  I  M  F  I  Y  Q  S  O
C  T  Z  J  I  I  S  C  O  L  R  J  S  A  W  U  X  Q  Y  R
M  B  Q  Q  P  T  F  E  I  Y  N  K  T  Q  F  L  T  U  T  B
I  A  M  M  Q  A  R  H  C  P  V  D  I  W  K  V  R  V  P  A
L  L  Z  J  U  Q  Z  U  E  E  Q  I  V  Y  Q  Y  I  J  S  I
A  L  V  A  I  U  Z  W  M  W  V  X  T  F  M  Y  C  Q  U  I
N  E  X  P  W  R  X  B  D  Z  L  U  E  M  Y  R  K  S  Z  U
M  R  Y  R  B  M  H  U  K  E  Q  W  N  P  O  N  S  B  J  M
N  K  M  L  K  S  U  B  Q  Y  I  H  P  F  C  G  T  T  W  L
J  X  Q  O  W  K  G  O  A  L  S  C  O  R  E  R  E  A  R  G
C  J  U  Y  M  I  D  F  I  E  L  D  E  R  K  X  R  H  E  J
```

FOOTBALLER	RIGHTFOOTED	ACMILAN
TRICKSTER	SKILL	MIDFIELDER
ASSIST	FLAMENGO	GOALSCORER
BARCELONA		

CHAPTER

5

WORLD CUP DISAPPOINTMENT AND OLYMPIC BRONZE MEDAL

"Ronaldinho lacks an important characteristic of Maradona and Pele – aggression. They transformed themselves in adversity. They became possessed, and furious."
- Tostao

On March 29, 2003, Ronaldinho scored a goal to level the game at 1-1, but Brazil still lost 2-1 to Portugal in a friendly game at Estadio das Antas, Porto. He made three appearances at the 2003 FIFA Confederations Cup but could not score a single goal as Brazil crashed out in the group stage. On September 10, he scored the only goal to help Brazil to a 1-0 win over Ecuador in a 2006 FIFA World Cup qualifier.

Ronaldinho scored Brazil's last goal in a 4-1 win over Hungary in a friendly game at Ferenc Puskas Stadium, Budapest on April 28, 2004. Brazil coach Carlos Alberto Pereira left him out of the squad for the 2004 Copa America, opting to take mostly fringe players. Brazil still went on to win the tournament, beating Argentina 4-2 on penalties after a 2-2 draw in the final. Ronaldinho returned to the team with a bang, scoring a hattrick in a 6-0 win over Haiti in a friendly game played at the Stade Sylvio Cator, Port-au Prince, Haiti, on August 18, 2004. He also netted Brazil's second goal in a 3-1 home win over Bolivia in a 2006 FIFA World Cup qualifier on September 5, as well as the equalizing goal of a 1-1 draw with Germany in a friendly game on September 8.

On February 9, 2005, Ronaldinho scored Brazil's fourth goal in a 7-1 win over Hong Kong at Hong Kong Stadium. He netted Brazil's first two goals in a 4-1 home win over Paraguay in a 2006 FIFA World Cup qualifier on June 5. After his two goals, he captained Brazil to glory at the 2005 FIFA Confederations Cup in Germany, chipping in with goals against Japan in the group stage, Germany in the semifinal, and Argentina in the final. In the same game, he was named Man of the Match following Brazil's 4-1 win. His three goals, added to the six he scored at the 1999 edition of the tournament ranks him as the competition's all-time joint-highest goal scorer with 9 goals, level with Mexican forward Cuauhtémoc Blanco.

Ronaldinho was included in Brazil's 23-man squad for the 2006 FIFA World Cup as part of a much-hyped attacking lineup that featured Ronaldo, Kaka, and Adriano, who were together expected to bring to the fore the "Joga Bonito" style of play that was the subject of widespread advertising campaigns by top brands such as Nike in the build-up to the tournament. Ronaldinho himself was at the height of his powers at the time, having just won a second successive FIFA World Player of the Year and a first Ballon d'Or after leading Barcelona to an impressive double of La Liga and the UEFA Champions League.

But Brazil, labeled "top heavy and unbalanced" flattered to deceive, and crashed out after a surprising 1-0 loss to France in the quarterfinals where the five-time winners could only muster one attempt on target. Ronaldinho's only goal involvement at the tournament was his assist for Gilberto's goal in a 4-1 win over Japan in the group stage.

The team received severe criticism from the media and Brazilian fans following their return home. Two days after the loss to France, a 23-foot tall fiberglass and resin statue of Ronaldinho in Chapeco, erected to celebrate his 2004 FIFA Player of the Year award win, was vandalized and destroyed. On the same day, Ronaldinho, joined by Adriano on his return to Barcelona, held parties at his house and at a nightclub. This worsened the feelings of Brazilian fans, who believed they had been cheated through a lack of effort from the squad of superstars. Brazil's underwhelming performance at the 2006 FIFA World Cup is now viewed by many as the turning point of his career, the moment that signaled the end of his reign at the very top of the game.

On March 24, 2007, Ronaldinho ended his scoreless international streak that had lasted nearly two years with a brace in Brazil's 4-0 win over Chile in a friendly game in Gothenburg, Sweden. Due to fatigue, he requested to be left out of the squad for the 2007 Copa America, which Brazil still won. He returned to the team with a goal in a 2-0 win over Algeria in a friendly game in Montpellier, France, on August 22. On September 9, Ronaldinho put Brazil 3-2 up in a 4-2 win over USA in a friendly game at Soldier Field Stadium in Chicago. His last competitive goal for Brazil's senior national football team was scored on October 17, 2007, in a 5-0 win over Ecuador in a 2010 FIFA World Cup qualifier.

On July 7, 2008, Ronaldinho was included as one of the three overage players in Brazil's squad for the 2008 Summer Olympics. Though Barcelona initially moved to stop his participation as it clashed with the club's involvement in the 2008-09 UEFA Champions League playoff round, his path was cleared following his transfer to AC Milan in July 2007, as the Serie A side had no objections to his participation at the quadrennial event. Ronaldinho scored a goal in two warm-up friendly games the team played before the start of the Games. At the 2008 Summer Olympics Football event, Ronaldinho was appointed as Brazil's captain, and he featured in all six games his team played, scoring two goals in a 5-0 win over New Zealand in the group stage. Nevertheless, Brazil crashed out of the competition in the semifinals following a 3-0 loss to eventual winners, Argentina. In the third-place playoff, Brazil defeated Belgium 3-0 to pick up the bronze medal.

Ahead of the 2010 FIFA World Cup, Ronaldinho recaptured some of his good form and was included in the provisional 30-man squad submitted to FIFA on May

11, 2010, but he was dropped from the 23-man final squad by Brazil coach Dunga. Critics asserted that the exclusion of superstars like Ronaldo, Ronaldinho, Adriano, and Alexandre Pato suggested a departure from the traditional Brazilian offensive-minded "Joga Bonito" style of play. At the 2010 World Cup in South Africa, Brazil finished top of a group that contained Portugal and Cote d'Ivoire and made light work of Chile with a 3-0 victory in the round of 16. Robinho put the South Americans 1-0 up in the quarterfinal clash with the Netherlands before two well-taken strikes from Dutch midfielder Wesley Sneijder sent Brazil crashing out of the tournament.

Ronaldinho returned to the national fold in September 2011 under new coach, Mano Menezes, in a friendly game against Ghana played at Craven Cottage, West London. He played for the entire duration of the game as his team won 1-0. He had two impressive performances in successive friendlies against Argentina in October, before scoring his last international goal in a 2-1 win over Mexico in a friendly game at Estadio Corona, Torreon, Mexico, on October 11.

Still in good form in 2013, Ronaldinho received a call up from Brazil coach Luiz Felipe Scolari for a friendly game against England on February 6, 2013, as part of activities to commemorate the 150th anniversary of the English Football Association. Ronaldinho was included in Brazil's starting lineup for the match. As the game progressed, Dinho had a chance to score from a penalty kick, but his effort was saved by English keeper, Joe Hart, as Brazil suffered a 2-1 defeat. He also received another call up for a friendly against Chile on April 24, 2013, a match he started as captain. Ronaldinho's international career effectively ended after he was omitted from Brazil's squad for the 2013 FIFA Confederations Cup, and the 2014 FIFA World Cup, both being held in his native Brazil. He played 97 official senior international matches and scored 33 goals.

10 Trivia questions

1. How many appearances did Ronaldinho make at the 2003 FIFA
    Confederations Cup?

    A. 5

    B. 4

    C. 3

    D. 2

2. Which team did Ronaldinho score a hat-trick against in 2004?

    A. Hungary

    B. Bolivia

    C. Germany

    D. Haiti

3. How many goals did Ronaldinho score at the 2005 FIFA Confederations Cup?

    A. 2

    B. 3

    C. 4

    D. 5

4. Ronaldinho's only goal involvement at the 2006 FIFA World Cup was an assist. Who was the beneficiary?

    A. Gilberto

    B. Adriano

    C. Kaka

    D. Ronaldo

5. Ronaldinho ended a scoreless streak that had lasted nearly two years with goals in March 2007. Who were the opponents?

    A. Argentina

    B. Bolivia

    C. Chile

    D. Denmark

6. Which team did Ronaldinho score his last competitive goal for Brazil against?

    A. Austria

    B. Belgium

    C. Canada

    D. Ecuador

7. How many goals did Ronaldinho score at the 2008 Summer Olympics Football event?

    A. 1

    B. 2

    C. 3

    D. 4

8. Who were the opponents when Ronaldinho scored his last international goal?

    A. Mexico

    B. USA

    C. Ghana

    D. England

9. Which England keeper saved Ronaldinho's penalty in February 2013?

    A. Ben Foster

    B. David James

    C. Joe Hart

    D. Jordan Pickford

10. How many senior international goals did Ronaldinho score?

    A. 30

    B. 31

    C. 32

    D. 33

10 Trivia Answers

1. C – 3

2. D – Haiti

3. B – 3

4. A – Gilberto

5. C – Chile

6. D – Ecuador

7. B – 2

8. A – Mexico

9. C – Joe Hart

10. D – 33

RONALDINHO MAZE #2

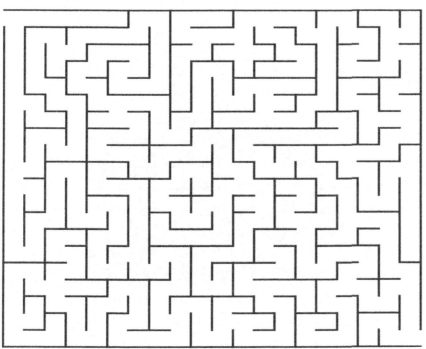

GOAL

CHAPTER

6

RECAPTURING FORM AT MILAN AND BRAZIL

"The decline of Ronaldinho hasn't surprised me. His physical condition has always been very precarious. His talent though, has never been in question."
– Carlo Ancelotti

Before they signed his compatriot Robinho in late August, Manchester City offered Barcelona £25.5 million for Ronaldinho in July 2008, but Ronaldinho rejected the move despite the £200,000 per week salary that came with the offer. Instead, he opted to join his Brazil teammate Ronaldo at AC Milan, who sealed a deal with Barcelona for €24.15 Million, while offering a salary package of €6.5 million per year to the player. As the number 10 shirt he had become used to wearing was occupied by Dutch legend Clarence Seedorf, Ronaldinho went for jersey number 80.

Ronaldinho made his competitive AC Milan debut on August 31, 2008, when he was named in the starting lineup for a home Serie A game against Bologna. He played the whole 90 minutes of a 1-2 loss for his side. His first goal for the club came as the winning goal of a 1-0 Milan derby win over rivals Inter on September 28. On October 19, he netted a brace in AC Milan's 3-0 win over Sampdoria, and scored the winning goal in injury time during a 1-0 UEFA Cup win over SC Braga on November 6.

After his satisfactory start, Ronaldinho struggled with fitness issues later in the season, resulting in many appearances off the bench. For his perceived lack of dedication to training and lifestyle of late-night partying, he received criticism from then AC Milan coach, Carlo Ancelotti. He finished a disappointing first season with 10 goals in 32 appearances across all competitions, which included 8 goals in 29 Serie A games.

Ronaldinho began to recapture some of his good form in the 2009-10 season under new coach, Leonardo, who moved him from the central midfield role he had assumed under Ancelotti to a more familiar left-sided forward role in an attacking 4-3-3 setup. His first goal of the season came as an equalizer in a 1-1 Serie A draw at Atalanta, after he had been introduced as a substitute. In the next league game, he scored the winning goal from the penalty spot to help AC Milan to a 2-1 home win over Roma. He also netted an equalizer in a 1-1 home draw with Real Madrid in a UEFA Champions League group stage game.

On January 10, 2010, Ronaldinho netted a brace to help AC Milan win 3-0 away at Juventus. A week later, he bagged his first hattrick for the club in a 4-0 win over Siena. In a UEFA Champions League round of 16 first leg match against Manchester United in mid-February, Ronaldinho put AC Milan ahead early on with a deflected effort in the third minute of the game, though the English side rallied back to claim a 3-2 away win. Ronaldinho scored the winner from a penalty kick in a 1-0 win over Fiorentina in May, before he netted another brace in a 3-0 win over Juventus in the last AC Milan's last Serie A game of the season. He finished the season with 15 goals in 45 appearances across all competitions, despite missing three penalty kicks. He also had the most assists in Serie A with 13.

The 2010-11 season turned out to be Ronaldinho's last at AC Milan. In the first half of the season, he featured in a new-look attack that consisted of new recruits, Robinho and Zlatan Ibrahimović. Before his departure from the club in January 2011, he made 16 appearances across all competitions and scored his only goal for AC Milan that season in a 2-0 win over Auxerre in the UEFA Champions League group stage. He left AC Milan after making 95 appearances and scoring 26 goals.

Despite being linked with a transfer back to his boyhood club, Gremio, alongside a host of other clubs like Corinthians, Palmeiras, LA Galaxy and Blackburn Rovers, Ronaldinho agreed a move to Flamengo on a contract expected to last until the end of the 2014 season. More than 20,000 fans attended his presentation, after he was unveiled on January 12, 2011. He scored his first goal for the club in a 3-2 win over Boavista on February 6. Three weeks later, he scored a second half free kick to help Flamengo to a 1-0 win over Boavista and secure the Taca Guanabara, his first piece of silverware with Flamengo.

In April 2011, Ronaldinho added another trophy to his collection when Flamengo won the Taca Rio. On July 27, Flamengo went 3-0 down inside the first half hour of a game away at rivals Santos, before Ronaldinho scored a hattrick to help his side to a 5-4 comeback win. He finished the 2011 season with 21 goals in 52 appearances across all competitions. After he had been absent from the club for a few days, Ronaldinho sued Flamengo on May 31, 2012, alleging that the club had not paid him for, while also voiding his contract with the club. By the time he was ready to leave Flamengo, Ronaldinho had scored 28 goals in 72 appearances across all competitions for the club.

Four days after he had canceled his contract with Flamengo, Ronaldinho joined Atletico Mineiro on a six-month contract, starting from June 4, 2012. As his favored jersey number 10 was already occupied by Guilherme, he chose number 49 as his shirt number, in reference to his mother's birth year.

Ronaldinho made his debut for Atlético Mineiro on June 9, and played the whole 90 minutes of a 1-0 win at Palmeiras. He scored his first goal for the club from a penalty kick in a 5-1 win over Nautico on June 23. His first hat-trick for the club came in a 6-0 home league win over Figueirense SC. He led the club to a respectable second-place finish in the Campeonato Brasileiro Série A, an achievement that earned the club a place in the 2013 Copa Libertadores. He finished the season with 9 goals in 32 appearances across all competitions and was awarded the Bola de Ouro award as the league's best player in 2012.

In the 2013 season, Ronaldinho led Atlético Mineiro to the Campeonato Mineiro and the club's first Copa Libertadores title, scoring four goals and providing eight assists in an eventful continental triumph. He finished the 2013 season with 17 goals in 38 appearances across all competitions, and was deservedly voted as the 2013 South American Footballer of the Year. He also scored two goals from free kicks at the 2013 FIFA Club World Cup. His first goal was the equalizer in a 3-1 defeat to Raja Casablanca in the semifinal, while the second also leveled the score at 2-2 in a 3-2 win over Guangzhou Evergrande in the third-place playoff. Ronaldinho renewed his contract with Atletico Mineiro in January 2014, but after adding the Recopa Sudamericana to his list of honors, he found an agreement with the club to terminate his contract in July 2014.

On September 5, 2014, Ronaldinho agreed to join Mexican side Queretaro on a two-year contract. He made his debut for the club in a 1-0 defeat to Tigres UANL, a game in which he missed a penalty kick. In his next game, he scored from a penalty and provided an assist to Camilo Sanvezzo in a 4-1 win over Chivas Guadalajara. He scored a consolation goal from a free kick in a 2-1 defeat to Atlas at the Estadio Jalisco on October 30, before netting a brace in a 4-0 away win over CF America at the Estadio Azteca on April 18. He received a standing ovation from the crowd that comprised mostly of CF America fans, a gesture that moved him to tears.

Ronaldinho scored two penalties in two successive games, the second being the winning goal in a game against Chiapas FC that secured a place for Queretaro in the Liga MX playoffs. On May 17, 2015, Ronaldinho scored from a free-kick in a 2-2 draw with Tiburones Rojos de Veracruz, a result that gave his club a 4-3 aggregate victory and a place in the semifinals. Queretaro advanced to the finals at the expense of Pachuca after the semifinal tie had ended 2-2 on aggregate. Queretaro lost the final 5-3 on aggregate despite a 3-0 second leg win, as they had lost 5-0 in the first leg. At the age of 35 in June 2015, Ronaldinho revealed his decision to leave Queretaro and offered his gratitude to Queretaro fans and the rest of Mexico. He scored 8 goals in 29 appearances across all competitions for Queretaro.

On July 11, 2015, Ronaldinho disclosed his return to the Brazilian top flight after agreeing an 18-month contract with Fluminense. He did not score a goal in the nine appearances across all the competitions he made for the club, before his contract was terminated by mutual consent on September 28 due to poor form that drew intense criticism from fans. He played a few futsal games in India between 2016 and 2017, before announcing his retirement from football on January 16, 2018.

10 Trivia questions

1. What jersey number did Ronaldinho pick upon his arrival at AC Milan?

   A. 10

   B. 70

   C. 80

   D. 90

2. Who did Ronaldinho make his competitive AC Milan debut against?

   A. Atalanta

   B. Bologna

   C. Chievo

   D. Genoa

3. When Ronaldinho scored his first goal for AC Milan, who were the opponents?

   A. Juventus

   B. Sampdoria

   C. Udinese

   D. Inter Milan

4. How many league goals did Ronaldinho score in his first season at AC Milan?

   A. 8

   B. 9

   C. 10

   D. 11

5. In which season did Ronaldinho score a goal for AC Milan against Real Madrid?

   A. 2008-09

   B. 2009-10

   C. 2010-11

   D. 2011-12

6. Who did Ronaldinho score his first hat-trick for AC Milan against?

   A. Palermo

   B. Cagliari

   C. Siena

   D. Napoli

7. How many league goals did Ronaldinho score against Juventus during the 2009-10 season?

   A. 4

   B. 0

   C. 2

   D. 1

8. In July 2011, Ronaldinho scored a hattrick for Flamengo. Who were the opponents?

   A. Botafogo

   B. Palmeiras

   C. Fluminense

   D. Santos

9. How many goals did Ronaldinho score for Atletico Mineiro at the 2013 FIFA Club World Cup?

    A. 4

    B. 3

    C. 2

    D. 1

10. How many appearances did Ronaldinho make across all competitions for Queretaro?

    A. 30

    B. 29

    C. 28

    D. 27

10 Trivia Answers

1. C – 80

2. B – Bologna

3. D – Inter Milan

4. A – 8

5. B – 2009-10

6. C – Siena

7. A – 4

8. D – Santos

9. C – 2

10. B - 29

RONALDINHO WORD SEARCH #3

```
T Z U H N O I M U G R A B J B D R T S K
Q S V V D G Z P E L A F P T P B I I O P
S N A X R K E K C H F T Y P S I C R U K
I Y U I P A R I S I M Q J J Y L M N T E
J S K G Y W L P O R T O A L E G R E H I
Y S L J N O T M H F W L H K M A Z H A A
L E J W G A S H E Z G N M Y N T I Q M D
B J S T U D B P P O D O V V N L S D E K
T P J H E I W O R L D C U P K E A D R P
Z F C E D W B B O N Z Q V C D T X C I M
J W Y W H B S E L A D R I P L I L N C P
G E H I M U C S Y K H X K Z F C Q O A B
W W M Z Y J A Q M P V Q H Y N O P L T T
L K F A F H B S P D E G H Y H M S N C C
L F L R M Y N T I S Q H P Z M I H H M Y
I H A D F U V U C M S W C D Q N E D R W
C I I S Z B H Q S W A Y Y J W E M I E L
L B R C O P A A M E R I C A H I O K E A
H Q O B F L U M I N E N S E X R P Z V U
S Y O Z I Z S P D G I X P E V O I B D G
```

ATLETICOMINEIRO   COPAAMERICA   THEWIZARD

FLUMINENSE   PARIS   FLAIR

WORLDCUP   PORTOALEGRE   OLYMPICS

SOUTHAMERICA

CHAPTER

7

CAREER ACHIEVEMENTS

"Ronaldinho is total class – a very, very great player."
– Zinedine Zidane

Ronaldinho is one of the most-decorated players of all-time, being one of only nine players that have won the FIFA World Cup, UEFA Champions League, and the Ballon d'Or. He belongs to an even smaller group of players that have won the Copa Libertadores alongside the aforementioned three honors. He began collecting silverware at only 17 years old, when he won the 1999 South American U-17 Championship and the FIFA Under-17 World Championship with Brazil. A couple of years later, he won the Copa Sul and Campeonato Gaucho with boyhood club Gremio.

Ronaldinho won the Copa America in 1999, the FIFA World Cup in 2002, and the FIFA Confederations Cup in 2005. He has also won the CONMEBOL Pre-Olympic Tournament in 2000, and was part of the Brazil team that won a bronze medal at the 2008 Summer Olympics. At Barcelona, Ronaldinho won two La Liga titles, the Supercopa de Espana twice and the UEFA Champions League once. He won the Campeonato Carioca at Flamengo, before adding the Campeonato Carioca, Copa Libertadores, and Recopa Sudamericana during a successful spell at Atletico Mineiro.

Ronaldinho has also won a lot of individual accolades during his illustrious career. In 1997, he was awarded the Bronze Ball at the FIFA Under-17 World Championship. In 1999, he was named in the South American Team of the Year, finished as top goal scorer in the Campeonato Gaucho, and received the Golden Ball and Golden Shoe awards at the 1999 FIFA Confederations Cup. In 2000, he won the Bola de Prata and finished as top goal scorer in the CONMEBOL Pre-Olympic Tournament.

Ronaldinho was named in the FIFA World Cup All-Star Team in 2002, won the Ligue 1 Goal of the Year award in 2003, and was named in the FIFA 100 in 2004. He received the Don Balon Award in 2003-04 and 2005-06, and the Trofeo EFE in 2003-04. He won both the FIFA World Player of the Year and FIFPro World Player of the Year awards in 2005 and 2006, and was named in the UEFA Team of the Year from 2004 to 2006. In 2005, Ronaldinho claimed both the Ballon d'Or and Onze d'Or awards, as well as the Bronze Ball at the 2005 FIFA Confederations Cup.

World Soccer Magazine named Ronaldinho as its Player of the Year in 2004 and 2005. He was also named UEFA Club Forward of the Year in 2004-05, and UEFA Club Footballer of the Year in 2005-06. From 2005 to 2007, Ronaldinho was named in the FIFPro World XI. He finished as top assist provider in both La Liga and the

UEFA Champions League in the 2005-06 season, and came third in the 2006 FIFA World Player of the Year.

In 2009, Ronaldinho received the prestigious Golden Foot Award and was named in the Sports Illustrated Team of the Decade. He finished as Serie A top assist provider in the 2009-10 season, and won his second and third Bola de Prata awards in 2011 and 2012. Ronaldinho received the Bola de Ouro award in 2012, and was named Campeonato Brasileiro Serie A Best Fans Player, and included in the Campeonato Brasileiro Série A Team of the Year for 2011 and 2012.

Ronaldinho finished as top assist provider in the Campeonato Brasileiro Série A in 2012, and in the Copa Libertadores in 2012 and 2013. He was named as South American Footballer of the Year in 2013, and finished as top goal scorer at the 2013 FIFA Club World Cup. Ronaldinho was included as a substitute in the UEFA Ultimate Team of the Year published in 2015, and in the Ballon d'Or Dream Team (Silver) announced in 2020. In 2021, he received the Player Career Award at the Globe Soccer Awards. He has also been inducted into the Brazilian Football Museum Hall of Fame and the AC Milan Hall of Fame. Ronaldinho is the joint all-time highest goal scorer of the now defunct FIFA Confederations Cup with 9 goals.

10 Trivia questions

1. In what year did Ronaldinho win the highly coveted Ballon d'Or award?

   A. 2004

   B. 2005

   C. 2006

   D. 2007

2. Which award did Ronaldinho receive at the 1997 FIFA Under-17 World Championship?

   A. Golden Ball

   B. Silver Ball

   C. Bronze Boot

   D. Bronze Ball

3. With which Brazilian club did Ronaldinho win the Copa Libertadores?

   A. Gremio

   B. Flamengo

   C. Atletico Mineiro

   D. Internacional

4. On how many occassions did Ronaldinho win the FIFA World Player of the Year?

    A. 1

    B. 2

    C. 3

    D. 4

5. In what year did Ronaldinho win the FIFA Confederations Cup?

    A. 1999

    B. 2003

    C. 2005

    D. 2009

6. On how many occasions was Ronaldinho named in the FIFPro World XI?

    A. 3

    B. 2

    C. 1

    D. 0

7. In what year did Ronaldinho receive the prestigious Golden Foot Award?

    A. 2006

    B. 2007

    C. 2008

    D. 2009

8. At the end of which season was Ronaldinho named UEFA Club Footballer of the Year?

    A. 2003-04

    B. 2004-05

    C. 2005-06

    D. 2006-07

9. On how many occasions was Ronaldinho named South American Footballer of the Year?

    A. 0

    B. 1

    C. 2

    D. 3

10. How many trophies did Ronaldinho win with Barcelona?

    A. 5

    B. 6

    C. 7

    D. 8

10 Trivia Answers

1. B – 2005

2. D – Bronze Ball

3. C – Atletico Mineiro

4. B – 2

5. C – 2005

6. A – 3

7. D – 2009

8. C – 2005-06

9. B – 1

10. A – 5

RONALDINHO CROSSWORD #1

Across

[2] AC Milan team colors

[3] His second Brazilian Club

[5] National Team

[6] AC Milan stadium

Down

[1] Position

[2] LaLiga Club

[4] Serie A Club

[7] Preferred Foot

CHAPTER

8

PERSONAL LIFE

"My dad gave me some of the best advice I've ever had. Off the field, he told me to do the right thing and be an honest, straight-up person."
- Ronaldinho

R onaldinho has a son from his ex-wife, Brazilian dancer, Janaina Mendes. He met her after the 2002 FIFA World Cup, and they dated for a couple of years before getting married in 2004. They had Joao, named after Ronaldinho's late father, on February 25, 2005. The marriage ended in 2007, the same year Ronaldinho gained Spanish citizenship. Ronaldinho has also dated several other women, such as Lisa Collins and Ximena Capristo. Between 2006 and 2008, he had a relationship with French model Alexandra Paressant, and between 2010 and 2011, he dated Sara Tommasi. In January 2017, Ronaldinho courted controversy when it was reported that he had proposed to marry both Priscilla Coelho and Beatriz Souza.

Ronaldinho's most notable hobby outside football during his career was attending the biggest and wildest carnivals in Brazil or partying at home and in nightclubs. He once had an accident while attending his mother's birthday celebrations in Porto Alegre. His SUV car, driven by his personal driver, fell into a ditch, but both escaped unhurt. Ronaldinho is a self-acclaimed car fanatic and has been seen many times driving exotic cars during his career. Ronaldinho is a Catholic Christian, and has been seen offering prayers several times before the start of football matches. His favorite food is Feijoada, often cooked for him by his mother. Besides football, he enjoys basketball, and his favorite singer is Jorge Aragao. He also prefers Pro Evolution Soccer to other football video games.

Ronaldinho had a sponsorship contract with sportswear and equipment manufacturer Nike, and endorsement deals with brands like Pepsi, Coca Cola, EA Sports, Gatorade, and Danone, among others. He featured in an advert for Nike in 2005, in which he was given a new pair of Nike boots with which he repeatedly hit volleys against the crossbar, retrieving the ball each time before it touched the ground. The recorded clip of the ad was the first to reach one million views on YouTube. He earned about $20 million from endorsement deals alone in 2006, and appeared in commercials with a number of his Brazil teammates, as well as other superstars like Thierry Henry, David Beckham, and Lionel Messi. Ronaldinho entered into an endorsement deal with Coca Cola in 2011, but the deal was terminated in July 2012 when he brought a Pepsi to a media briefing. In February 2017, FC Barcelona revealed that they had agreed a 10-year contract with Ronaldinho to represent the club as an ambassador at institutional functions.

Ronaldinho has also made a number of contributions towards charitable efforts.

In 2005, he partnered with the World Food Program, and in 2006, he started a school in his hometown of Porto Alegre. He was appointed a UNAIDS ambassador in 2011, and in 2018, he captained a team during the 'Match for Solidarity,' a charity match held in Switzerland to raise funds and spread awareness about the UEFA Foundation for Children. In March 2018, Ronaldinho joined the Brazilian Republican Party, which had ties to the Universal Church of the Kingdom of God. During the 2018 Brazilian presidential election, he threw his weight behind eventual winner, Jair Bolsonaro.

In July 2019, Ronaldinho had dozens of his properties as well as his Brazilian and Spanish passport seized by Brazilian authorities due to unpaid fines and taxes. The fine, which was imposed after Ronaldinho built a fishing platform on Guaiba River in a 'heritage-protected' area, was eventually reduced by a judge from R$8.5 million to R$6 million. After Ronaldinho and his brother failed to pay the fines within a stipulated period, their passports were blocked.

In March 2020, Ronaldinho and his brother were questioned and arrested by Paraguayan authorities for using fake passports to enter the country. The brothers were detained at Paraguay's maximum security Agrupacion Especializada prison for 32 days before they were released on bail. Ronaldinho claimed the passports were given to him as a gift by a local sponsor, and that he made an innocent mistake of using it to gain entrance to the country. While under detention, Ronaldinho played in a futsal match, where he scored five goals and provided six assists to help his team to an 11-2 win. Ronaldinho and his brother were released from prison on April 7, and kept under house arrest in a hotel pending the payment of $1.6 million bail fee. The trial ended in August, and Ronaldinho and his brother were ordered to pay fines of $90,000 and $110,000, respectively.

10 Trivia questions

1. How many children does Ronaldinho have?

    A. 3

    B. 2

    C. 1

    D. 0

2. Which of these women had a child with Ronaldinho?

    A. Ximena Capristo

    B. Lisa Collins

    C. Sara Tommasi

    D. Janaina Mendes

3. Which sportswear manufacturer had a sponsorship agreement with Ronaldinho?

    A. Adidas

    B. Nike

    C. Puma

    D. New Balance

4. In what year did Ronaldinho become an ambassador for Barcelona?

    A. 2017

    B. 2018

    C. 2019

    D. 2020

5. In what year did Ronaldinho become UNAID's ambassador?

    A. 2010

    B. 2011

    C. 2012

    D. 2013

6. When did Ronaldinho join the Brazilian Republican Party?

    A. 2020

    B. 2019

    C. 2018

    D. 2017

7. For how many days was Ronaldinho detained in a Paraguayan prison?

    A. 10

    B. 12

    C. 22

    D. 32

8. In what year was Ronaldinho's properties and passports seized?

    A. 2020

    B. 2019

    C. 2018

    D. 2017

9. When did Ronaldinho participate in the 'Match for Solidarity'?

    A. 2018

    B. 2019

    C. 2020

    D. 2021

10. On what day was Ronaldinho released from Paraguayan prison?

    A.   April 15, 2020

    B.   April 6, 2021

    C.   April 7, 2020

    D.   April 18, 2021

10 Trivia Answers

1. C – 1

2. D – Janaina Mendes

3. B – Nike

4. A – 2017

5. B – 2011

6. C – 2018

7. D – 32

8. B – 2019

9. A – 2018

10. C – April 7, 2020

RONALDINHO CROSSWORD #2

Across

[2] Barcelona's stadium
[7] First ever goal for Brazil
[8] Birth city

Down

[1] The year he transferred to Barcelona
[3] His kit number at AC Milan
[4] First senior debut team
[5] His coach at Barcelona
[6] The year he transferred to AC Milan

PUZZLE SOLUTIONS

RONALDINHO'S MAZE #1

RONALDINHO'S WORD SEARCH #1

```
E H I H E O S G L I C A M P N O U N R Y
C V M W R G W Z C C H P C Q W B K O Y P
W X N D P Z Q O L Y Q S U L A H U X K B
C O C G C O R A D K F N Q S E R I E A F
H O U Z R R K M X P L A L E Y E K W F I
A I D A L B J O N Q O X I W I N G E R R
M I D W N I B A L L O N D O R D J J G J
P D S L N A Q C J C J T O X F B I F J G
I V L D K F P N Z A Q M I M I E I I L I
O B H J F W K D L I X J Z R M M N W I J
N L A L I G A P G L J C A T F I B J V F
S Z M E Z D T K W C R H H L T Q J L Q K
L K H A D F V M E U A J V S A N S I R O
E O P N R O N A L D I N H O O R Q D P W
A V Z F X W J Y I T M R O S S O N E R I
G S Q N O B U U X Y E O S A Z E T F S I
U T Z P B R A Z I L W H O L W E Y E L W
E X N H U T W T E S C O N S K X N I P U
A J J K K V N T E J V W A R T J V P Q Q
W C X O W L U O L X W E T J P O K G S E
```

RONALDINHO	SERIEA	WINGER
ROSSONERI	SANSIRO	LALIGA
CAMPNOU	BRAZIL	BALLONDOR
CHAMPIONSLEAGUE		

RONALDINHO'S WORD SCRAMBLE #1

1. KLULFLIS ILEBDRBR   SKILLFUL DRIBBLER

2. EAIVTERC RASSPE   CREATIVE PASSER

3. YAAMOBTNLF SYLET   FLAMBOYANT STYLE

4. RSRTICTEK NCIGAMIA   TRICKSTER MAGICIAN

5. YAPKNLIGAM NSGEUI   PLAYMAKING GENIUS

6. NEBTPEIRDULAC EOSMV   UNPREDICTABLE MOVES

7. PES-RLWNGCIDAO SRTCIK   CROWD-PLEASING TRICKS

8. -CEKRKEIF LAETISSICP   FREE-KICK SPECIALIST

9. STSIAS AESTRM   ASSIST MASTER

10. FUOJYL HSCRMAIA   JOYFUL CHARISMA

11. ASMBA ILFRA   SAMBA FLAIR

12. TSTNSIAHUCIE ILMSE   ENTHUSIASTIC SMILE

13. GAOJ IOBTON   JOGA BONITO

14. FRELEASS CTRAKTAE   FEARLESS ATTACKER

15. TLRNAUA MAOWHNS   NATURAL SHOWMAN

16. IVNIEENTV YPLA   INVENTIVE PLAY

17. DFVEEISEN SUEPRSER   DEFENSIVE PRESSURE

18. GEEANTL ABLL NCOOLTR   ELEGANT BALL CONTROL

19. CUKIQ WOOKOTRF   QUICK FOOTWORK

20. GOBLAL NCOI   GLOBAL ICON

RONALDINHO'S MAZE #2

```
Z  A  P  S  I  C  P  L  J  N  Q  B  A  R  C  E  L  O  N  A
L  S  T  L  V  R  Q  U  F  Y  B  S  J  X  T  H  K  X  I  M
X  B  G  U  W  M  S  B  S  Q  P  C  S  G  A  P  L  V  I  F
F  J  P  E  W  N  K  X  S  Z  K  C  A  R  A  T  H  J  L  L
I  C  R  I  G  H  T  F  O  O  T  E  D  J  R  H  Z  G  W  A
P  O  F  O  Y  S  C  S  J  H  X  A  K  P  G  C  U  E  F  M
K  T  G  G  M  Q  F  K  O  X  X  B  A  G  P  Z  G  X  T  E
V  F  P  N  J  M  O  I  S  L  L  N  S  P  T  F  Y  P  T  N
T  O  L  K  Y  F  Q  L  B  I  K  A  S  M  J  V  P  U  Y  G
A  O  C  X  I  D  N  L  J  X  S  D  I  M  F  I  Y  Q  S  O
C  T  Z  J  I  I  S  C  O  L  R  J  S  A  W  U  X  Q  Y  R
M  B  Q  Q  P  T  F  E  I  Y  N  K  T  Q  F  L  T  U  T  B
I  A  M  M  Q  A  R  H  C  P  V  D  I  W  K  V  R  V  P  A
L  L  Z  J  U  Q  Z  U  E  E  Q  I  V  Y  Q  Y  I  J  S  I
A  L  V  A  I  U  Z  W  M  W  V  X  T  F  M  Y  C  Q  U  I
N  E  X  P  W  R  X  B  D  Z  L  U  E  M  Y  R  K  S  Z  U
M  R  Y  R  B  M  H  U  K  E  Q  W  N  P  O  N  S  B  J  M
N  K  M  L  K  S  U  B  Q  Y  I  H  P  F  C  G  T  T  W  L
J  X  Q  O  W  K  G  O  A  L  S  C  O  R  E  R  E  A  R  G
C  J  U  Y  M  I  D  F  I  E  L  D  E  R  K  X  R  H  E  J
```

FOOTBALLER	RIGHTFOOTED	ACMILAN
TRICKSTER	SKILL	MIDFIELDER
ASSIST	FLAMENGO	GOALSCORER
BARCELONA		

RONALDINHO'S MAZE #2

RONALDINHO'S WORD SEARCH #2

```
T Z U H N O I M U G R A B J B D R T S K
Q S V V D G Z P E L A F P T P B I I O P
S N A X R K E K C H F T Y P S I C R U K
I Y U I P A R I S I M Q J J Y L M N T E
J S K G Y W L P O R T O A L E G R E H I
Y S L J N O T M H F W L H K M A Z H A A
L E J W G A S H E Z G N M Y N T I Q M D
B J S T U D B P P O D O V V N L S D E K
T P J H E I W O R L D C U P K E A D R P
Z F C E D W B B O N Z Q V C D T X C I M
J W Y W H B S E L A D R I P L I L N C P
G E H I M U C S Y K H X K Z F C Q O A B
W W M Z Y J A Q M P V Q H Y N O P L T T
L K F A F H B S P D E G H Y H M S N C C
L F L R M Y N T I S Q H P Z M I H H M Y
I H A D F U V U C M S W C D Q N E D R W
C I I S Z B H Q S W A Y Y J W E M I E L
L B R C O P A A M E R I C A H I O K E A
H Q O B F L U M I N E N S E X R P Z V U
S Y O Z I Z S P D G I X P E V O I B D G
```

ATLETICOMINEIRO   COPAAMERICA   THEWIZARD

FLUMINENSE   PARIS   FLAIR

WORLDCUP   PORTOALEGRE   OLYMPICS

RONALDINHO'S CROSSWORD PUZZLE #1

```
                              ¹M
                               I
   ²B  L  A  C  K  A  N  D  R  E  D
    A                      F
    R                      I
    C        ³F  ⁴A  M  E  N  G  O
    E            C        L
⁵B  R  A  Z  I  L        M        D
    O            I        E
    N            L        R
    A            A
            ⁶S  A  N  S  I  ⁷R  O
                           I
                           G
                           H
                           T
```

RONALDINHO'S CROSSWORD PUZZLE #2

Down:
1. TWOTHOUSANDTHREE
4. GREMII
5. FRAKIJKAARD
3. EIGHY
6. TWENTYEIGHT

Across:
2. CAMPNOU
7. NINETEENNINETYNINE
8. PORTOALEGRE

FINAL WHISTLE

Hello our fellow footBaller.

We really hope you enjoyed *The Best Ronaldinho Trivia Book Ever*. And, congratulations on reading it to the end!

We create these books to allow football fans to expand their knowledge around their favorite clubs and players, but most importantly, to keep the passion we all have for the game lit and alive.

Life can come with many challenges and setbacks. But something that never leaves our side is our love for the game.

If you enjoyed reading this book, we'd like to kindly ask for your feedback and thoughts in the review section on Amazon.

This would really encourage us to keep creating the highest quality books and content for football fans across the globe.

>> Scan the QR Code above to leave a short review <<

Thanks in advance!

Ball out,

The House of Ballers team.

Printed in Great Britain
by Amazon

35367526R00046